A New True Book

JAPAN

By Karen Jacobsen

*This "true book" was prepared
under the direction of
Illa Podendorf,
formerly with the Laboratory School,
University of Chicago*

CHILDRENS PRESS™

CHICAGO

Noh dance at a shrine

PHOTO CREDITS

Japan National Tourist Organization: Cover, 2, 7, 8, 10 (3 photos), 13, 18, 21, 22 (2 photos), 23, 24, 26, 29 (left), 31 (right), 32, 35 (top), 37 (2 photos), 38 (2 photos), 40, 42 (3 photos), 43.
Colour Library International: 4, 12, 15, 16, 20, 29 (right), 31 (left), 35 (bottom), 44 (3 photos).
Cover: The Garden of a Feudal Lord

Library of Congress Cataloging in Publication Data

Jacobsen, Karen.
  Japan.

  (A New true book)
  Includes index.
  Summary: Photographs and text present the physical geography, history, and culture of the "land of the rising sun."
  1. Japan—Juvenile literature. [1. Japan]
I. Title.
DS806.J148   952   82-4445
ISBN 0-516-01630-X   AACR2

TABLE OF CONTENTS

Mount Myoko (me • YO • ko) and Lake Nojiri (no • JEER • ee)

THE LAND

Japan is a beautiful country. It lies just off the eastern coast of Asia.

Japan is the first country to see the sun rise in the morning. That is why Japan is known as "the land of the rising sun."

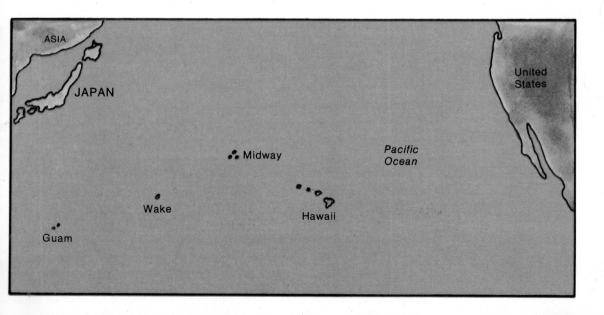

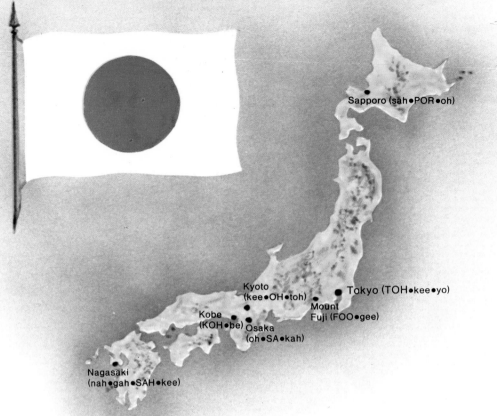

Japan is a nation of islands. There are four large islands and more than 3,000 smaller ones. The large islands are Hokkaido, Honshu, Shikoku, and Kyushu.

A snow sculpture at the Sapporo (sah • POR • oh) Snow Festival. Sapporo is on the island of Hokkaido.

Hokkaido has a cold climate. In winter more than ten feet of snow falls on Hokkaido. There are some small farms on Hokkaido. But most of the island is not farmed.

The city of Nagasaki (na • ga • SAH • kee) is on the island of Kyushu.

Kyushu is in southern Japan. It has very mild weather.

Nagasaki is one of the biggest cities on the island. Many ships are built here.

Shikoku is the smallest of Japan's main islands. It has springs, mountain forests, and waterside hotels. Shikoku is just across the Inland Sea from Honshu, the largest of Japan's islands.

Shoppers on
city street in
Tokyo (TOH • kee • oh)

Traffic
in Toyko

Marunouchi (mar • oo • NOO • chee)
business center
in Tokyo

TOKYO

More than one hundred million people live in Japan. They live mainly in cities.

Tokyo is the largest city. It is on the island of Honshu. It has more than ten million people. It is one of the largest cities in the world.

Tokyo is also the capital of Japan. It is a very busy city.

THE SEACOAST

Japan has thousands of miles of beautiful seacoast. In the fall, strong wind and rain storms, called typhoons, cause heavy damage to coastal towns.

THE MOUNTAINS

Mountains cover most of Japan's land.

Some of the mountains are volcanoes. The highest, named Mount Fuji, is a quiet volcano.

Mount Fuji
(FOO • gee)

Japan also has many earthquakes. Most are weak, but a strong earthquake may cause great damage.

The Japanese have learned to make buildings that can stand up to typhoons and earthquakes.

Isobe (ih • SOH • bay) Village, with the Japanese Alps in the background

FARMING AND FISHING

Because of its mountains, Japan does not have much farmland. To grow as much rice, fruit, and vegetables as possible, the Japanese use every bit of land, even the sides of mountains.

Fishing boats, freighters, and barges in Kobe (KOH • bay) Port

Japanese fishing boats go all over the world. They catch tons of fish from the sea.

THE PEOPLE OF JAPAN

Japan has very old customs or rules. They are a part of everyday life.

The most important rules are about the family. Japanese young people are expected to respect their parents.

In Japan, people wear both traditional and western clothes.

It is very common in Japan for three generations—grandparents, parents, and children—to live together in the same house. The grandparents are loved and respected.

Today Japan is changing. The old rules are not always followed. But most Japanese people combine the best of the old ways with the best of the new.

Yunomaru
(yoo • no • MA • roo)
Farm

HOMES

On a farm the whole family works together.

In the city the father may go to work. The mother may work, too, or she may stay home to care for young children.

More than eight million people live in Osaka (oh • SAH • ka) on Honshu Island.

In cities people live in modern apartments. They are heated by gas or electricity. Almost every home in Japan has a television and a telephone.

High-speed trains carry people from one city to another.

Above: Yoshimura (yo•shih•MOO•ra) Mansion, Osaka

Left: Row of old houses in the city of Takayama (ta•ka•YAH•ma)

Some Japanese live in three- or four-room houses. The roofs are covered with tiles. The outer walls are made of wood. The inside walls are made of sliding paper panels.

A girl wearing a kimono prepares tea according to the rules set down. This tea ceremony is hundreds of years old.

Woven mats, called tatami, cover the floors. By day cushions serve as seats. At night special pads, called futons, are placed on the floor for sleeping.

Tokonoma (toh • koh • NO • ma)

Almost every home has
a special corner, called a
tokonoma. The tokonoma is
decorated with flowers and
a painting. This corner
shows the beauty of
nature.

FOOD

Most Japanese food is fried, boiled or broiled. Pieces of fish, chicken, pork, or beef are often cooked with vegetables in soy sauce.

For hundreds of years tea has been a favorite drink. Today the Japanese drink whatever they wish. But most Japanese still drink tea with their meals.

Sukiyaki (soo • kee • YAH • kee) being served in a traditional Japanese inn.

The Japanese use chopsticks to eat. Rice is a part of every meal.

EDUCATION

Education is free in Japan. Starting at age six every child must attend six years of primary school and three years of junior high school.

Most students go on to three years of high school. Good students can go to four years of college or university.

Education is very important. The students work hard. They know that a good education leads to a good job in Japan.

In school Japanese children learn to read and write Japanese.

Japanese is not hard to speak.

Above: Japanese grocery store

Left: Children learn to draw Japanese characters.

But Japanese is very hard to write. Each word is written in a special way. There are thousands of words and thousands of characters and letters to be learned.

JAPAN'S PAST

Japanese children also learn the history of their country. Japan has a long history.

More than 1,300 years ago Prince Shotoku ruled Japan. This leader brought Chinese writing, art, dress, and religion into Japan.

The shoguns (generals) ruled in the name of the emperor until 1867. They often lived in castles (left) and kept warriors (right) to fight for them.

In 1192 Yoritomo Minamoto became shogun, the ruler of all Japan. For almost 700 years Japan was ruled by shoguns.

Imperial Palace in Tokyo is the home of the emperor of Japan.

JAPAN TODAY

Today, Emperor Hirohito is the royal leader of Japan. But he has no real power. He is more like a father to his people.

Japan is ruled by elected officers. The leader of the government is the Prime Minister.

Modern Japan is strong. Its people are busy. They work hard. They make many things—cars, ships, steel, TVs, radios, and cameras. They sell them everywhere in the world.

The Japanese turn holidays into a special treat for the family.

One favorite holiday is Kodomo-no-Hi or Children's Day on May 5. On this day gaily painted paper or cloth fish are flown from poles—one fish for each son.

Carp streamers fly on Children's Day. The carp is a symbol of courage and perserverance.

Children wear kimonos during a Cherry Blossom Festival.

The favorite sport in Japan is baseball.

The Japanese have many sports. Kendo is a type of fencing with long sticks.

Judo and karate are popular, too.

Sumo wrestling is a very old sport. Sumo wrestlers weigh about 300 pounds.

Left: Sumo wrestlers
Above: Skier racing downhill.

Japanese athletes win gold medals in contests all over the world.

Many Japanese people like exercise. Swimming, hiking, and boating are popular. In winter thousands of Japanese go skiing.

Bunraku puppets are big.

Puppet shows are very popular. Puppet shows are given in parks, market places, and puppet theaters.

The most famous puppets in Japan are the Bunraku. They have beautiful costumes and are almost the size of a small child. It takes three puppeteers to work each Bunraku puppet.

Kabuki began more than 350 years ago.

Live actors perform
Japanese plays that have
been popular for hundreds
of years. Male actors play
all the parts—even women's
parts. They wear makeup
and beautiful costumes.

Most of the people know the plays by heart. Still they laugh and cry at every play.

The Japanese also like to see modern plays. Television and movies are very popular, too.

Japanese artists have created many beautiful art objects:
Above: Japanese vase
Below right: Lacquerware is often made in small, family-owned businesses.
Below left: Three beautiful women of Edo (EE•doh), a painting by Utamaro
(oo•ta•MAH•roh)

Artist paints the face of puppet

For hundreds of years Japanese artists have made beautiful paintings, baskets, pottery, and textiles. Today Japanese arts and crafts are sold all over the world.

Bamboo grove

Golden Pavilion, Kyoto

Snow-covered
farmhouse
with thatched
roof

44

The Japanese make many new and useful products, fast and well. These, too, are sold all over the world.

Life in modern Japan is good. Work is very important. But sport, art, and the enjoyment of natural beauty are a part of everyone's life, too. In Japan the sun rises on a beautiful and busy land.

WORDS YOU SHOULD KNOW

Asia(AlJ • eh) — the largest continent on Earth.

Bunraku(bun • RAH • koo) — famous Japanese puppets that are almost life-size.

capital(KAP • ih • tal) — a city where the government is located.

combine(kum • BYNE) — to bring together; to join.

custom(KUSS • tum) — a rule that a group of people live by.

earthquake(ERTH • kwaik) — a shaking of the ground caused by sudden movement of rocks underneath the Earth's surface.

elect(ee • LEKT) — to vote for someone or something.

emperor(EM • per • er) — a person who rules an empire.

futon(FOO • tahn) — a pad that is used in Japan to sleep on.

generation(jen • er • RAY • shun) — a period of about 30 years; the time between the birth of parents and the birth of their children.

honor(ON • er) — to respect.

judo(JOO • doh) — a sport practiced by people in Japan.

karate(ka • RAH • teh) — a sport started in Japan where the hands and feet are used as weapons.

kendo(KEN • doh) — a sport in Japan where long sticks are used as weapons.

kimono(kih • MOE • no) — a long, loose robe with wide sleeves that is worn by people in Japan.

lacquerware(LACK • er • wair) — wooden objects coated with a varnish.

mild(MYLD) — neither very hot nor very cold.

obey(oh • BAY) — to listen to; to follow an order or request.

panel(PAN • ihl) — a part of a wall that can be moved.

pavilion(pah • VILL • yun) — a building that has a pointed roof, and often has open sides.

perseverance(per • se • VER • ence) — doing something in spite of difficulties.

respect(ree • SPEKT) — to honor; to treat well.

shogun(SHOW • goon) — the general who ruled Japan in past years.

sumo wrestling(SOO • moh RESS • ling) — a sport of Japan practiced by very heavy men.

tatami(tah • TAH • mee) — a mat put on the floor in homes in Japan.

textile(TEX • tyle) — a woven cloth.

tile(TYLE) — a material used to make a roof.

tokonoma(toh • koh • NO • mah) — a place in a Japanese home set aside to show the beauty of nature.

traditional(tra • DISH • un • el) — following a custom.

typhoon(tye • FOON) — a kind of hurricane with strong winds and heavy rains.

university(yoon • ih • VERSS • ih • tee) — a school that is made up of colleges.

volcano(vahl • KAY • noh) — an opening in the earth's crust through which lava, dust, ash, and hot gases are thrown.

INDEX

About the Author

Karen Jacobsen is a graduate of the University of Connecticut and Syracuse University. She has been a teacher and is a writer. She likes to find out about interesting subjects and then write about them.